THE GOSPEL

GOD'S GAMEPLAN FOR THE CHRISTIAN LIFE

Wallace Francis and Ed Ellis

LifeSource Creations Publishing

LifeSource Essentials Ministries, Inc. / LifeSource Creations Publishing
P. O. Box 1109
Cumming, GA 30028
www.wfimc89.com

Book Layout © 2014 BookDesignTemplates.com
Cover Design by Janice Ellis
Cover Graphics: CanStock Photo

The Gospel/ Wallace Francis and Ed Ellis
ISBN 978-0-9908762-6-7

Dedication

"AND THIS <u>IS</u> ETERNAL LIFE THAT THEY
MAY KNOW THEE,
THE ONLY TRUE GOD, AND JESUS CHRIST
WHOM THOU HAST SENT."

JOHN 17:3

When this passing world is done,

When has sunk yon glorious sun,

When we stand with Christ on high,

Looking o'er life's history;

Then, Lord, shall I fully know, not till then—how much I owe.

–Robert Murray McCheyne

Table of Contents

Acknowledgments

The authors would like to give special thanks to those faithful friends, brothers and sisters, who generously gave of their time, talents, and unique perspectives to read the raw manuscript and suggest the changes and refinements that helped make this GOSPEL presentation the tool we hope it will be to the Church of our Lord Jesus Christ.

Among this faithful band we want to thank John and Jan P., Kevin D., Jeff O., Jeff G., Jerry and Gerri W., Derry C., Gary G., Dan J., Warren P., Ralph D., Bill C., Dave H.

Special thanks to my daughter, Abigail, who gave me the critically important insight: "If you want to engage men, especially young men, don't ask them a yes or no question—because all you will get is a yes or no! Also, to my dear wife, Janice, who is responsible for all the cover designs and editing labors, without her, none of our books would be possible. Her treasure is in heaven.

Ed Ellis

Introduction

This year, tens of thousands of young boys all over America will run around chalk-lined grass fields playing football. Over one million high schoolers will line up on either side of the scrimmage line each year, many dreaming of scoring the game-winning touchdown that leads to a championship season. Yet, of this million-plus army that plays football in high school, only 1/10 of 1% will end up playing professional football in the NFL—that's roughly one out of 1000.

It's a game which in many ways is simple enough for a child to play, yet it can be so demanding of skill, sacrifice, and commitment that only a few can reach the highest levels. But the offer and the opportunity is open and available to everyone who wants to play.

While it is by no means a perfect analogy, the offer of the gospel of Jesus Christ is similar in many ways.

It is simple enough for a child to respond to the call to follow Jesus Christ, yet so challenging that many who hear the call turn away at what they think is too high a price. How can both be true?

The key to the child's response is found in his simplicity and transparency. Children don't have much, if anything, invested in their life in this world. They are not yet deceived by the lies this world appears to offer for success, opportunity, and prosperity. They are not yet hardened by the pain, suffering, and disappointments which will surely come. They willingly acknowledge their failures to "do right" and do not try to hide their fear of punishment.

Possibly the greatest advantage they enjoy is that they can be easily entreated. Their first instinct is to believe and trust—not to doubt and refuse to believe.

The beauty of a little child's faith is that when he or she does trust you, it is done with a whole heart—the child doesn't know any other way. With older folks it's not so simple.

THE CHALLENGE TO THE CHURCH

A common challenge to the church in our day is the un-churched ("professing" believers and unbelievers alike) appear to be turning away from the traditional church—apparently believing it no longer has the answers for the ultimate questions in life that it once did. In other words, they do not see the message of the church as *relevant* to the world in which we live. That would mean that the gospel of Jesus Christ is not relevant today. Is that true?

Many pastors (some leading very large congregations) see this as a challenge, as well as an opportunity—even a man-date to do things differently. They want to attract as many unchurched people as they can. Their mantra is to be *seeker-friendly*. This is code for "do whatever you need to do in order to make the church as attractive and warm and com-fortable as possible"—making sure to avoid anything that might "turn them off."

Consequently, many have adopted media-driven worship services that rival world-class rock concerts and built facilities with amenities that would rival many of the most elite country clubs and resorts—and it's usually free! The truth is, it is often spellbindingly attractive!

And none of this is necessarily wrong. Jesus drew large crowds. The desert amenities weren't exactly world-class, but He could do miracles and healings that modern pastors simply can't do. He wasn't opposed to large crowds. He welcomed them and met their needs in awe-inspiring ways. Clearly, He had compassion for their needs and suffering and proved it by His healing miracles and miraculous provisions—but He also had another equally compelling motive.

He wanted people to come and hear His message. His miracles always had a larger purpose—they were meant to provide testimony to the **power** of His message to save them—to change their lives forever. That dramatic life-change could only come by trusting Him enough to turn from the direction they were going and to follow Him.

There is often one major, glaring difference between the "gospel" message of the modern church in America and the message Jesus preached to His multitudes.

Jesus gathered the crowds and then proclaimed a message about an eternal kingdom, the kingdom of God, in which there would be countless blessings—and nothing on earth could compare with them. There would be no more sorrow, pain, suffering—or death! It was a place of untold wealth and prosperity for all; a place where everyone enjoyed all the privileges of being part of the "royal family" (Revelation 21:4; Ephesians 1:18; Matthew 6:20; Philippians 4:19).

But the greatest blessing of all was intimate fellowship with God as our Father. Those who heard quickly realized this was truly good news. They literally hung onto every word—they wanted Him to be their King.

THE CHOICE

Eventually, Jesus also made it clear that to receive this blessing, you would have to make a choice—a choice between continuing to live your life for <u>your</u> sake, pursuing <u>your</u> goals and dreams in this world, or leaving them behind and deciding to trust the Lord Jesus and follow Him on a different path, one that would lead to the new kingdom He had promised.

One path leads to a new life; the other path leads to destruction. One path is narrow and often difficult to travel; the other path is wide and seems to offer great potential for success and earthly prosperity—but in the end, everyone on that path *dies.* All the promises were an illusion.

To those who would choose to follow Him, He assured them He would never leave them nor forsake them, and would provide all they needed to enter the kingdom of God (from the cross to the new birth)—and this life would never end!

To Jesus, this choice was as much a part of His gospel message as all the blessings it offered. But this part of His message often offended many of His would-be followers—and to the surprise of many, Jesus let them go. It is simply a fact, He never forces anyone to follow Him, but He does require them *to choose* whether or not they will follow Him.

Like a child, you simply had to believe Him, trust Him, and follow Him. But many had too much invested in <u>this</u> life—too many dreams and goals they still wanted to accomplish. They were unable to see past the delusions of their selfish ambitions for this life to the truth that it was all in vain. They wanted all the blessings that Christ offered, but they balked at the need to "deny themselves and take up their cross" to follow Him.

We wonder if those who are gathering the large crowds today are balking at preaching the <u>whole</u> gospel message that Jesus preached—the cross as well as the crown—for fear of losing the crowds. Jesus was not afraid—neither should we be afraid to do it His way. Our job is simply to be faithful—the results are up to Him. After all, isn't the church His bride—shouldn't He know how He wants to pursue her?

This book is an attempt to share the Gospel of Jesus Christ—the way Jesus did, and to prove once again that His Gospel is still **"the power of God unto salvation."**

The Ultimate Question in Life

The Ultimate Question in Life

Many people spend much of their lives trying to avoid the biggest question that each of us will ever face. What is it?

"Are you going to die?"

You might respond, "Of course, we're all going to die—you know, eventually." That's a comforting, generic, sort of "we're all in the same boat" answer. But that's not the question.

The question is, *"Are* **YOU** *going to die?"*

Of course, the answer is YES. But do you know *why* you are going to die?

Again, a lot of people might say they are going to die because of old age, cancer, or heart disease. But these are all just symptoms of a deeper root cause.

The Bible has a different answer; it tells us in no uncertain terms what the ultimate cause of death is. It says that *death* is God's punishment for sin. That puts death in a whole different light. Now it's a moral issue, not a physical issue. We die because of a moral deficiency. We die because we have lost our connection with the One who is the source of life.

Death was *never* in God's plan for us when He created us. Adam would never have died if he had not sinned. Death is not natural. We all know this. The strongest instinct we have is the will to survive. Death is an enemy we fight to the end. We know it's not the way things should be.

God's plan was for Adam to live with Him and enjoy Him—forever! But Adam rejected God's plan. Adam was deceived into believing that God was withholding His best from Adam and that there was a *better* plan for his life—a plan by which he could be *like* God, i.e., he could be his own god.

SIN—WHAT IS IT?

But Adam sinned...He disobeyed God's simple command, and because he did, "sin entered the world and <u>death</u> through sin" (Romans 5:12).

Sin and death always go together. They are the cause and effect of most of what goes on in this life. What then is SIN? It can have many forms. It can be a transgression, that is, a crossing over a known boundary. So is disobedience. We sin when we disobey any of God's commands. Ultimately, whenever we do any of these things, it means that we have fallen short of a standard established by a higher authority—in this case, God's standard—God's moral law.

Many miss this point. They may realize they fall short ("No one is perfect, right?"). But they console themselves with the thought that others do worse things than they do. In other words, they compare themselves with others and use that comparison to feel better about themselves. But the problem with this is, this is <u>not</u> the standard God uses.

What moral standard does God use? How does God judge us? God's standard is Himself, His own divine perfection. This is what the theologians rightly describe as His holiness. He has given us moral laws, objective standards of right and wrong that are consistent with His own righteous character—and which apply to everyone. To violate those laws is to "fall short of His glory." God is perfect (holy, pure, and righteous), and He can only dwell with those who are holy like Him.

You might respond, "That is an impossible standard!" That is absolutely true—now, but it wasn't when we were first created. When Adam was created, he was a perfect man. God delighted in him.

What did Adam do to deserve the punishment of death?

By disobeying the Creator's command (a very simple command not to eat of one tree), Adam destroyed the peace and harmony of God's creation. Through Adam and his rebellion against God's sovereign right to rule His creation, **SIN** entered the world. Death is God's punishment for sin.

At its core, **sin is rebellion**; it is man deciding to do his own will, pursue his own selfish desires and purposes *for* his life, rather than "honoring God as God" in his life and being grateful for the abundance of His blessings. Man has chosen to go his own way, to be god of his own life, and ruler of his own kingdom. There is no exception, we all continue to make the same choice Adam made.

Adam did not believe that he was accountable to God. He was wrong—and we have all inherited his selfish desire to rule his own life—to live to fulfill our own selfish desires. What we fail to see is this pursuit of the fulfillment of our selfish ambitions always ultimately ends the same way—in death!

The lure of lasting success in this life is all a delusion. Sadly, most people don't realize this until it's too late and our fate is sealed—forever. We have forgotten (or willfully ignored the fact) that we are God's creatures, not the Creator. God is God. We are not God...and we answer to Him.

JUDGMENT—WHY

Choices have consequences and the Bible is clear about the consequences of our sin and rebellion. "The wages of sin is death." There is no exception to this—"The soul that sins will die" (Romans 6:23; Ezekiel 18:4).

The sentence of death is <u>not</u> something about which God is unsettled, as if He is still considering *if* He will impose it on mankind. The issue of judgment against sin is settled— the wrath of God abides on us—now! John 3:18 unequivocally declares that the unbeliever is judged already.

At the moment of our physical death, not only the physical consequences, but also the eternal consequences of our sin will become permanent. This is why most people live in fear of death all their lives. They know in their hearts they will have to give an account for the selfish lives they have lived—and they have the dread sense it is not "good enough." They are right. Paul leaves no doubt in Romans 3:10, 23:

> "...There is **none** righteous, not even one."

"...**All** have sinned and fall short of the glory of God."

You will be judged for your sins; I will be judged for mine. Do you know where you—you personally—have fallen short? We all desperately want to believe that, deep down in our hearts, we are "good persons"—but the facts of our lives prove it's just not true (not if we use God's standard—and that is what He will use—the standard of perfection).

Have you ever asked yourself where you have fallen short? Have you ever stolen anything from anyone? Ever? Have you ever lied? Have you ever committed adultery or immorality or lusted after another person? Have you ever killed anyone? Been unjustly angry? Have you ever slandered anyone? Cheated anyone? The Spirit of God will gladly bring to your mind your particular failing, just ask Him for His help! It's His job.

That includes you and me. Where have <u>you</u> fallen short? Remember, even in the everyday world, you only have to steal or kill *once* and you become a thief or a murderer.

God's standard is even more demanding. Consider these questions, they cut to the core of the issue: Have you lived to do <u>your</u> will or God's will? Is your life's purpose to fulfill <u>your</u> goals, and <u>your</u> dreams, for <u>your</u> life, or (as Jesus Christ did) have you lived to do the Father's will? Jesus said,

> "Not everyone who says to Me, 'Lord, Lord,' will enter the kingdom of heaven; but he who does the will of my Father who is in heaven."
>
> (Matthew 7:21)

That is the standard. The truth is undeniable, we all fall short.

Man's predicament is hopeless...*unless* God intervenes.

"BUT GOD..."

One of the most majestic phrases in all the Scriptures is the phrase, "But God..." The wonderful truth is that God does know our plight and He has intervened. But why?

Why doesn't God simply end it all now and send us to hell forever...and just start over? The answer is as simple as it is profound...and well-known. God loves us. He does not desire that anyone should perish. He wants all men to repent (turn back <u>from</u> their rebellious, selfish lives) and turn back <u>to</u> Him, and seek His forgiveness (2 Peter 3:9).

He is willing to forgive us—and has made that forgiveness possible for all of us. But in order to make it possible for us to be forgiven of our sins and reconciled to God, He had to do something unthinkable.

What did He do?

Oh, teach me what it means;

That Cross uplifted high,

With One, the Man of Sorrows,

Condemned to bleed and die.

O teach me what it cost Thee to make a sinner whole;

And teach me, Savior, teach me the value of a soul.

—Lucy Bennett

Questions for the Huddle

From the Introduction—

1. Jesus often drew large crowds to hear His message.

    A. What was His message?

    B. Why was it important to them? Why could it change their lives?

    C. His message offered enormous blessings, but Jesus made it clear that there was a choice to be made. What was the choice?

From Section One—

1. Is the message of the Gospel an offer to ADD something to your life, or is it something which will transform your life? Which do you want?

2. Many, if not most, people believe they will die because of a physical weakness or disease.

    A. What is the real reason you will die?

    B. For what is the punishment of death?

3. Do you believe you are accountable to God for your life and decisions? Why or why not?

4. What determines your standing before a Holy God?

5. Do you believe you are a "good person"?

    A. If so, why? How do you measure "good"?

    b. What is God's standard?

6. How will God judge your answers to these questions?

Notes

_____

_____

_____

_____

_____

_____

_____

_____

_____

_____

_____

_____

_____

_____

_____

_____

_____

_____

_____

_____

_____

God's Side of Salvation

"While we were yet sinners, Christ died for us."

Romans 5:8

God's Side of Salvation

The Cross

God could not and did not arbitrarily decide to pardon us for our sin and rebellion. No righteous judge could do that. The righteous demands of His divine law had to be met—divine justice had to be satisfied. How could God accomplish this without pouring out His wrath against sin on us?

He did it by providing a substitute—by finding someone who would be willing **and** worthy to take our place and suffer the wrath and punishment of God against our sin and rebellion.

To be *worthy* in this sense means that He had to be sinless, both in action and character. The book of Hebrews describes the Lord Jesus this way—he was "holy, innocent, undefiled, separated from sinners..."—and eventually, "exalted above the heavens" (Hebrews 7:26).

Of course, this meant that Jesus would have to live a life just like we do, face the same temptations and trials that we do, and still not fall into sin. Only then could He or would He be considered a *worthy* sacrifice, sufficient to satisfy the justice and wrath of a holy God. Certainly, one of the most thrilling events in all of Scripture was the day when John the Baptist looked up and saw Jesus coming and could say to his disciples:

> "Behold, the Lamb of God who takes away the sin of the world!" (John 1:29).

And it is important to note, John pointed to a man—a man had to be able to accomplish this work. A man had to stand between God and man as our substitute, as our mediator, and endure the wrath of a holy God, if we were to be saved! One of Jesus' favorite descriptions of Himself was "the Son of Man."

There has ever been only one person who could fill that role—the Lord Jesus Christ. He was and is the unique being of the universe.

> "BEHOLD, THE VIRGIN SHALL BE WITH CHILD AND SHALL BEAR A SON, AND THEY SHALL CALL HIS NAME IMMANUEL," which translated means, "GOD WITH US" (Matthew 1:23).

He not only had to be good, He had to be perfect. He had to be both God **and** man in one unique person. Paul describes who it had to be in his first letter to Timothy:

> "For there is one God, and one mediator also between God and men, the man Christ Jesus, who gave Himself as a ransom for all, the testimony given at the proper time." (1Timothy2:5-6)

But even if such a unique person could be found, why in the world would He be willing to do what He did? The indignity and humiliation He endured? The lies and slander and injustice? The only possible answer is LOVE.

Only one person has ever loved God the Father more than Himself. There was only one person who had this kind of selfless love toward God the Father—His Son.

So God sent His Son, His only Son—His willing and worthy Son to take our punishment on Himself. He took our place when He died on the cross—"the just for the unjust"—the godly for the ungodly.

> "...He Himself bore our sins in His own body on the cross..." (I Peter 2:24).

On the cross, Jesus said, "It is finished" (John 19:30).

What did He mean?

The penalty for our sins was paid—paid in full. The barrier to divine blessing was removed—at least from God's side. Because of what Jesus did, the Father could forgive us for our sin and rebellion. On the positive side, as we will see, He was now free to pour out enormous blessings, beginning with our being adopted into the very family of God!

How do we know that Jesus' sacrifice of Himself for our sins was accepted in heaven, that it was enough to satisfy the wrath of a holy God? Because God—the One who is the Judge and who poured out His divine wrath against our sin on Jesus—He raised Him from the dead. That is how we know.

THE RESURRECTION

The foundational truth of all Christianity is the resurrection of Jesus Christ. If this is not true, none of it is true. If this is true, then all of it is true. There is no middle ground.

The Resurrection is a miracle event—there is no way around this. Christianity is a miracle religion. If you have a problem with this, then faith in Christ will be a very difficult challenge for you. The resurrection is the anchor of everything the Christian believes. If He is not alive, then our hope for salvation is foolishness.

Is there any practical, empirical evidence that this is true— that Jesus really rose from the dead? Or is it just a "blind leap of faith?"

The Bible records that over a period of forty days, there were literally *hundreds* of eyewitnesses who testified to seeing Him alive from the dead—many of these (including almost all the twelve apostles) ended up dying for their testimony to its truthfulness. Men don't die for something they know not to be true.

Why did God raise Him from the dead? Why could death not hold Jesus in its *death-grip* until the day of God's judgment like it holds everyone else?

Because Jesus had no sin for which He was accountable. He died for <u>our</u> sins, not His.

> "He (God) made Him who knew no sin to be sin for us..." (*New King James Version*, 2 Corinthians. 5:21).

"But God raised Him up again, putting an end to the agony of death, since it was impossible for Him to be held in its power" (Acts 2:24).

Why is the Resurrection so important?

It is because what Jesus Christ did on the cross is what makes *salvation* possible for us. It is critically important we know that what was accomplished on earth was accepted in heaven on our behalf.

The letter to the Hebrews again makes it clear when it says:

> "We have such a high priest...who does not need to offer up sacrifices, first for his own sins, and then for the sins of the people, because this He did once for all when He offered up Himself"
> (Hebrews 7:27).

> "Now the main point...is this: we have such a high priest, who has taken His seat at the right hand of the throne of the Majesty in the heavens..."
> (Hebrews 8:1).

This is why Paul began his explanation of the gospel in the letter to the Romans with the foundational declaration "...concerning His Son, who was born of a descendant of David according to the flesh, (his true humanity); who was declared the Son of God, (His true deity) with power by the resurrection from the dead, according to the divine Spirit of holiness, Jesus Christ our Lord..." (Romans. 1:3-4).

This marvelous work of God's grace toward us in Christ is what makes our justification possible, and by raising Him from the dead we know God has accepted His sacrifice as payment for our sins. As Paul says in Ephesians 1:7, "In Him we have redemption through His blood, the forgiveness of our trespasses, according to the riches of His grace."

Now God can deal with us *without* regard to our sin. Sin is no longer an obstacle to a relationship with God. So is that the end? Is that all there is to salvation? Is justification all there is to salvation? You might think so to hear the way some present the gospel today. But that is not what the Bible teaches us, and that surely is not what Jesus taught His followers.

How do we know? Because justification can't deliver the greatest promise of the gospel. What is that? Eternal Life!

> "This **is** eternal life that they may know You, the only true God, and Jesus Christ whom You have sent" (John 17:3).

Justification removes the barrier to the possibility of a living, vital, intimate relationship with God, but it does not provide the ability to come to know and love Him. There is nothing personal in it. It is a divine declaration. Justification is not the experience of fellowship with God that the gospel offers and which the apostles declared as the Christian's experience. This is the Apostle John's testimony in his first epistle:

> "...And the life was manifested, and we have seen and testify and proclaim to you the eternal life, which was with the Father and was manifested to us—that which we have seen and heard we proclaim to you also, so that you too may have fellowship with us; and indeed our fellowship is with the Father, and with His Son Jesus Christ" (1 John 1:2-3).

Eternal life is more than a life that lasts forever. Much more important, it is a life lived in intimate fellowship with God—forever!

If the gospel is more than simply justification, what then is *salvation?* The term is often used loosely and the focus is almost entirely on "getting you to heaven." As wonderful as that appears at first, is salvation just about me getting my sins forgiven and some kind of assurance of a free ticket to heaven, or is it more? What does it really mean to be *saved?*

As incredible as the promise and opportunity of the forgiveness of sins and our being reconciled to God through the death of His Son is—*it really is only the beginning* of the good news of the gospel.

Lord of all being, enthroned afar,

Thy glory flames from sun and star;

Centre and soul of every sphere,

Yet to each loving heart how near.

Grant us Thy truth to make us free,

And kindling hearts that burn for Thee,

Till all Thy living altars claim

One holy light, one heavenly flame.

—O. W. Holmes

Questions for the Huddle

1. The Cross and the Resurrection are the foundation of the Christian faith.

> A. What was required for Jesus Christ to be a "worthy" sacrifice?

> B. What made His life sufficient to pay the penalty for your sins?

> C. Did he die for the sins of the whole world?

2. There was only one person in the entire universe, in time or eternity, who could fill the role of Mediator and Savior between God and man—Jesus Christ.

> A. What do you think it meant for God to become man?

> B. Why would that have been a challenge for Him?

3. The Bible says that God became man—that "...the Word became flesh and dwelt among us..." (John 1:1).

> A. What does it mean to be the "God-man"?

> B. Is He still the God-man? Will He always be the God-man?

4. Why would Jesus do this? How does his sacrifice shape or change your understanding of what true love is?

5. Why is the resurrection of Jesus Christ the ultimate proof of the truth of the gospel? In other words, without the proof of the resurrection, why is there no foundation for the gospel—or our faith?

> A. What verses tell us this? (Romans 1:4, I Corinthians 15).

6. What is the goal of the gospel?

> A. Is it just about me getting my sins forgiven, or something more?

> B. What is needed to create in me the ability to have a living, personal relationship with God?

Notes

Justification Is Just the Beginning of the Gospel

"Much more...we shall be saved by His Life"

Romans 5:10

Justification Is Just the Beginning of the Gospel

The core concept in salvation is rescue. To be saved is, by definition, to be rescued. It's the idea that someone who finds themselves in a helpless, hopeless situation is found, rescued, and brought to safety. The one who is rescued is unable to offer anything more to his desperate situation than his need. The rescuer has to do it all.

Think of a person who has fallen off a ship and is drowning in the middle of the ocean. Unless the individual is planning to commit suicide, he quickly realizes he is powerless to help himself, and hopelessly doomed unless someone who is able does what is necessary to save him. Someone who cares whether he drowns or not has to act in order for him to be saved.

Ephesians 2:4-5, 8, describes us in our helpless state:

> "But **God,** being rich in mercy, because of His great love with which He loved us, even <u>when we were dead in our transgressions</u> (sins), made us alive together with Christ..."

"For by grace you been saved through faith; and that not of yourselves, it is the gift of God"...

Paul explains this further in Romans:

"**But God** demonstrates His own love towards us, in that <u>while we were yet sinners</u>, Christ died for us" (Romans 5: 8).

The penalty for our sins was paid by the death of Jesus on the cross. That is a wonderful truth. As we saw earlier, He is the *Lamb of God who takes away the sin of the world.*

But Paul does not stop there. He goes on in the next verse to explain something greater—in his mind, *much* greater.

"<u>Much</u> <u>more</u> then, having now been justified by His blood, we shall be saved from the wrath of God through Him.

"For if while we were enemies, we were reconciled to God through the death of His Son, <u>much</u> <u>more</u>, we shall be saved by His <u>life</u>" (Romans 5:9-10).

What does Paul mean? Twice he says, "Much more..." What could be more than our deliverance from the wrath of God?

He means that when Jesus died on the cross, He sacrificed His life to pay the redemption price for us, the penalty we would have had to pay for our sins and rebellion. That debt was settled, paid in full. This great sacrifice delivers us (at least potentially) from the wrath of God when He finally judges all mankind for their sin.

What else do we need?

We need a righteous standing before God. But how can that happen? We have only known a life of sin. God provided a solution. Remember, Jesus Christ was able to be our sin-bearer because of His sinless, righteous life. Not only did this free God to forgive us for our sin and rebellion, it also frees Him to count Jesus' righteousness as ours when we put our trust in Him.

As we began to see in the last section, this is what the theologians call *justification*. It's a legal concept. In more common terminology, it is used to describe a man being "right" or without offense either with God or another person. In other words, any offenses that may have been committed in the past have been atoned for and are no longer a barrier to their relationship. Graciously, God has even wiped out any record of our past sins!

Redemption, reconciliation, and the imputing (or counting) of Christ's righteousness as ours makes up the full measure of what justification means. It assures us a peace with God that can never be broken. God, in His love and mercy, made all this possible for us.

In theology, this is where we are considered reconciled to God through Jesus Christ—the point at which the righteous wrath of God against sin is declared to be satisfied and God is now able to treat us as if we had never sinned. This blood redemption "transaction" is between God the Father and the Son—we have no part in it—though we reap all the benefits of it when we place our faith and trust in Jesus Christ. This is what makes possible our redemption and the forgiveness of all our sin and rebellion—forever! Theologians call it "the atonement."

But justification is only a part of the blessing that comes to us through the gospel. Indeed, it is what God **had** to do (and which <u>only</u> God could do) to remove the barrier to all the many blessings He wishes to give His redeemed children.

Don't miss that point! God's work in justification is what removes the barrier to God's desire to bless us!

THE REAL PROBLEM—THE DIVINE SOLUTION

But there is still another problem—a serious problem. There is no change **in** us. We still lack the ability to have a living, spiritual relationship with God. We may be justified (declared righteous in the court of heaven) and forgiven of our sins, but we still have the same old selfish, fleshly nature as before. We are no more "alive to God," no more able to live for God or glorify Him than before. Justification does nothing to make us spiritually alive. For that we need something more. What do we need?

We need life, spiritual life. That's what dead men need most of all—life! God knew that. That is what He provided for us through the resurrection of Jesus Christ—not just evidence of Heaven's acceptance of a sacrifice for our sins (as wonderful as that is!)—but a new life. It's a life empowered by the very same Spirit that empowers the risen Christ. This new life can only come through a new birth, a heavenly birth. This is what Jesus said to Nicodemus:

> "Truly, truly, I say to you unless one is born from above, he cannot see the **kingdom of God...**"—for**ever** (John 3:3)!

> "Truly, truly, I say to you, unless one is born of water and the Spirit, he **cannot enter into the kingdom of God.** That which is born of flesh is

flesh, and that which is born of the Spirit is spirit" (John 3:5-6).

"The last Adam became a life-<u>giving</u> spirit" (I Corinthians 15:45b).

This new life, this eternal life is also the gift of God. The Spirit of God Himself comes to dwell in us and with us. This was the message of the early church...this was the way, the only way, to gain entrance into the eternal Kingdom of the Lord Jesus Christ. In other words, to live with the King in His kingdom, you have to have the King living in you!

You have to have the same mind and the same heart as the King. This part of the gospel message is often missing today.

THE GOSPEL OF THE KINGDOM

When the apostles preached the gospel to the first converts, there were two pillars to their message—the kingdom of God, and the death and resurrection of Jesus Christ.

For some puzzling reason, preachers today are quick to preach about the death and resurrection of the Lord, but they leave out the centerpiece of Jesus' message—the kingdom of God! Why? He didn't preach about His death and resurrection to them, He preached about the great opportunity to live with Him and the Father in His kingdom.

The *kingdom of God* was the core of Jesus' message—this was the message that stirred the multitudes to see the possibility of a different life! It was a message of hope. It was the opportunity to live in a place of eternal blessing—no more sorrows or suffering, no more tears—no more death!

It was the opportunity to live a life of joy, peace, and abundance. A life that they could only dream about—but it could *never* be a reality for them in this world.

He was offering them the opportunity to live in the eternal kingdom of heaven and enjoy the constant presence of God Himself—who wouldn't respond to that? To the great masses of slaves in the Roman Empire and the poor people of Israel, it sounded great! Almost too good to be true.

And that is still the offer to us today.

The resurrection of Jesus Christ was the miracle-proof that His offer was real. On the day of Pentecost, the apostle Peter declared to the multitude,

> "Men of Israel—Jesus, a man attested to you by God with miracles and wonders and signs which God performed through Him in your midst...this man...you nailed to a cross by the hands of godless men and put Him to death.
>
> "But God raised Him up again, putting an end to the agony of death, since it was impossible for Him to be held in its power."
>
> "...God has made Him both Lord and Christ—this Jesus whom you crucified" (Acts 2:22-24, 2:36).

The resurrection was Heaven's seal of approval on all the work of Christ and all the promises of His gospel. It was undeniable proof that this new kingdom was real.

With the problem of sin dealt with, God was now free to pour out His blessings on mankind. At least on those who would respond to His offer.

So, what is man's side to this? God has made all the provision possible; does man do nothing?

How does all this come alive in me? **What must I do to be saved?** What is my responsibility in responding to this truly amazing offer of salvation and the gift of eternal life? Some try to say that you do nothing? Is that true? Not at all.

Both the apostles, Peter and Paul, made it clear; we have to "obey the gospel" (2 Thessalonians 1:8, I Peter 4:17). In the next two sections, we will explain what this means.

Give me a sight, O Savior,

Of Thy wondrous love to me,

Of the love that brought Thee down to earth,

To die on Calvary.

Oh, make me understand it,

Help me to take it in,

What it meant to Thee, the Holy One,

To bear away my sin.

—K. A. M. Kelly

Questions for the Huddle

1. What does it mean to be "justified" before God?

    A. What does it accomplish?

    B. What does it not do?

2. If you don't have physical life, then we would say that you are dead.

    A. How does this apply spiritually?

    B. What does it mean to be spiritually alive?

    C. What does it mean to be spiritually dead?

3. What does it mean to say that the only way to get into the Kingdom of God is to be born into it?

Notes

_____

_____

_____

_____

_____

_____

_____

_____

_____

_____

_____

_____

_____

_____

_____

_____

_____

_____

_____

_____

Man's Side of Salvation (Part I)

"It is written...that repentance for forgiveness of sins should be proclaimed in His name to all the nations..."

Luke 24:47

Man's Side of Salvation (Part I)

There are three essentials necessary if we are to have a biblical experience of God's saving grace in salvation. God is the source of all three, and while they are all normally experienced together in a single moment of time, they are also clearly distinguishable. These three essentials are repentance, faith, and a new birth.

REPENTANCE AND FAITH

The first essential in a true salvation experience is what the Bible calls *repentance*.

Before Jesus began His ministry, John the Baptist went before Him to prepare the way. His entire ministry was focused on one thing—preaching to the people "repentance for the forgiveness of sins."

When Jesus began His ministry, Mark 1 says that He came into Galilee preaching the gospel of God, and saying,

"The time is fulfilled, and the kingdom of God is at hand; repent and believe in the gospel" (Mark 1:15).

WHAT IS REPENTANCE?

Repentance is a word that is used over and over by Jesus, Peter, and Paul as the key to the *preparation* of a heart to receive the salvation which the gospel offers.

The common understanding of **repent** is **to turn away from** or **to turn back from** something or a path you are following. In basic biblical terms, it means a "change of mind"—that is, a change of mind which leads to a change in action and/or purpose. The Bible often uses it to describe the point at which a person "turns to God from idols to serve the living and true God" (I Thessalonians 1:9b).

Or, as in the Sermon on the Mount, it is described as turning from the *broad way* to follow Christ on the *narrow way* that leads to God—and to eternal life.

The entire ministry of John the Baptist was given to urging men to *repent* of their sins so they might be prepared for the coming of Jesus Christ. Similarly, on the day of Pentecost, the Bible says that those who heard his message were "pricked to the heart." Why? Because of the guilt and condemnation they felt when they realized they had actually participated in executing their own Messiah. When asked what they should do, Peter urged them to "repent" and seek God's mercy and forgiveness.

It was one of those amazing paradoxes of Scripture that the only way to find forgiveness was from the One they had rejected and crucified. It's true for all of us. Jesus said:

> "**I am the way,** and the truth and the life. No man comes to the Father except **through Me**" (John 14:6).

How humbling, how fearful it is when a soul realizes that the only way for it to be saved is to seek salvation from the One whom it has rejected all its life—the very One to whom that soul has refused to surrender and obey is its only hope!

The amazing truth of Scripture is that God wants us to come to Him—and has promised us complete forgiveness if we will come!

Hear His promises; He leaves no doubt:

> "All that the Father gives Me will come to Me, and the one who comes to Me I will certainly <u>not</u> cast out" (John 6:37).

> "I love those who love me; and those who diligently seek Me <u>will</u> find Me" (Proverbs 8:17).

> "You <u>will</u> seek Me and find Me when you search for Me with all your heart" (Jeremiah 29:13).

The questions rarely asked, but which are so crucial are:

Do I <u>really</u> want my old life to end? Is it really so bad? Am I convinced of my sin and guilt? Do I really deserve eternal punishment? Do I see my need for a Savior?

Or, do I just want God to clean up my life enough so I can go on like I was before, but not feel bad about it—and not be concerned about the eternal consequences?

My attitude towards repentance reveals my true heart.

REPENTANCE IS A CHOICE

In the Sermon on the Mount, the Lord Jesus made it clear that every person must choose his/her path in life—and there are only two choices: *a broad way* and a *narrow way.*

Most people choose the broad way. The fact is, we all start off on the broad way—it's the path that seems to offer us the most pleasure and fulfillment for <u>our</u> goals and desires. It's the path that allows us to rule and direct our lives. It appears to offer us the "freedom" to do whatever we want, whenever we want to. We are in control.

The problem, says the Lord Jesus Christ, is that this path which seems so wide and seems to offer such opportunity actually "leads to destruction, and many are those who enter by it."

Then He says some truly *terrifying* words: "For the gate is <u>small</u>, and the way is <u>narrow</u> that leads to life (eternal life), and <u>few</u> are those who find it" (Matthew 7:13b-14).

The critical question in every life is the decision to turn from the "broad way" to follow Jesus Christ on the "narrow way." Do we really want this new life? Do we really see that our old life is going to end up destroying us? The truth is, most do not see it—or refuse to believe it.

Most people look at their lives and think, "I admit, my life may not be all that it should be. I've made mistakes; there are some choices I regret—but if a few things were cleaned up (or cleaned out or made right), then my life might be acceptable to God and I could go on doing what <u>I</u> want to do."

Such people are not looking for biblical salvation; they want renovation—they want to clean out some things and re-fresh others.

But the truth is, like Lot's wife, they still love their <u>old</u> life and really do not want to leave it behind—*just clean it up so they feel better about it.*

They want to bring some of the *narrow way* onto the *broad way*—but they have no desire to give up the *broad way*. Just as the Bible warns, they still *love the darkness* of their old life. But God is light...and in Him there is no darkness at all. Light and darkness cannot dwell together.

It doesn't work. God won't let it work! He paid too high a price to secure our salvation. You can't serve two masters. You cannot serve yourself and God. You must choose the path you will follow. Every path has a destiny.

To choose the path is to choose the destiny—and the con-sequences are not optional, they are unavoidable.

Jesus' word to such people was very clear and simple: "If any man wishes to come after Me, he must deny himself, take up his cross daily, and follow Me" (Luke 9:23).

Part of repentance is understanding the need for turning from our sin—the need for a new beginning, a new life. One of the ministries which the Spirit of God performs in saving a lost soul is to convince and convict that person of his or her sin and rebellion. Only He can open the eyes of a deceived soul so that he sees and realizes he stands guilty and condemned before a holy God.

As important as it is to "turn from" our sin and rebellion, it is equally important to "turn to" God in child-like faith and trust. Repentance can't save us, it was never intended to save us.

Only Jesus Christ and what He accomplished for us can save us. The issue is this: until we are willing to repent, until we see the need to repent, and until we repent, we will never be in a position to turn to Jesus in saving faith. Jesus made this clear—

> "...but unless you repent, you will all likewise perish." (Luke 13:5b)

Oh, worship the Lord in the beauty of holiness,

Bow down before Him, His glory proclaim;

With gold of obedience, and incense of lowliness,

Kneel and adore Him; the Lord is His Name.

Fear not to enter His courts in the slenderness

Of the poor wealth thou wouldst reckon as thine;

Truth in its beauty, and love in its tenderness,

These are the offerings to lay on His shrine.

—J. S. B. Monsell

Questions for the Huddle

1. Why is repentance essential to salvation?

2. What does true repentance mean? Define repentance.

3. What is the fundamental choice in repentance?

4. Why is repentance not a "work" (that earns merit towards salvation)?

Notes

Man's Side of Salvation (Part II)

"...by grace are you saved through faith..."

Ephesians 2:8

Man's Side of Salvation (Part II)

SAVING FAITH

The second essential in a true salvation experience is **faith**. The apostle Paul said in Ephesians 2:8, we are saved "by grace through faith." Three times in the New Testament the declaration is made that "the just (justified) shall live by faith." In other words, there is nothing that can be added to faith in order to be saved. How then do repentance and faith go together?

It's like being a farmer. The farmer has to plow the soil to prepare it to receive the seed. If he doesn't do this, the soil will be "hard" and the seed won't be able to take root and grow into a harvest.

To use another simple analogy, faith is the back side of the "coin" of salvation, repentance is the front side. All throughout history men have used coins as legal tender in their commercial dealings with one another. If you look at a silver dollar, it will always have a head on one side and something else on the other. All coins have a head and a tail. If one or the other is missing, no one will accept that coin as legal tender; it is fraudulent, it has no value.

The same is true of repentance and faith. You need both to experience biblical salvation. That's what the Bible teaches—Jesus, Peter, and Paul all taught it. Repentance includes the awakening of the sinner to the guilt, condemnation, and consequences of his sin and rebellion against God, and the need of a Savior. Faith then secures the blessings the Savior offers in the gospel. Together they result in salvation—what the Bible calls *conversion*. Jesus told His disciples:

> "Truly I say to you, unless you are **converted** and become like children, you will <u>not</u> <u>enter</u> the kingdom of <u>heaven</u>." (Matthew 18:3).

The essence of true faith is **trust**. There is an important distinction between merely believing and truly trusting. You can believe in facts in the sense that you intellectually accept them as true, but this does not result in conversion.

Why not?

You may accept as truth the **fact** that Jesus died on the cross, and that He miraculously rose from the dead after three days—but believing these facts doesn't convert you into a Christian, any more than believing in Satan turns you into a devil!

Nor does believing in the devil turn you into a devil worshipper. The issue is what you <u>**do**</u> with the facts. The demons believe the facts (and even tremble!), but that doesn't result in their salvation. They don't repent, nor do they become followers of Christ.

Biblical faith is a <u>trust</u> commitment. It means committing something valuable to you into the care and keeping of someone you trust. The apostle Paul described this in his own life to his faithful co-worker Timothy in 2 Timothy 1:12b when he said,

> "I know <u>whom</u> I have believed (i.e., the Lord Jesus Christ) and am convinced (fully persuaded) that <u>He</u> is able to keep (guard/protect) that which I have entrusted (personally committed) to Him (my soul, my life, my eternal destiny) until that day."

To entrust means to give up control to another. The one to whom something is entrusted becomes the guardian, the protector of what is entrusted to him. He embraces it as his own personal responsibility. That is why the saved soul is eternally secure in the omnipotent hands of God our Savior. We entrust our souls to God Himself (John 10:28-29).

THE APOSTLE PAUL'S EXPERIENCE

When did this happen for the apostle Paul? In one of the more dramatic *conversion* experiences ever recorded, the Lord Jesus personally appeared to Paul while he was on his way to Damascus, fully intending to root out and destroy the "Christian heresy" wherever he found it.

Instead, he came face-to-face with the risen, glorified Son of God. This was Paul's "Oh, no!" moment. When he asked Him, "Who art Thou, Lord?" and heard the words, "I am Jesus,"—this was when he realized that everything he had believed and to which he had committed himself as a devout Jew and one of Israel's religious elite—was worthless.

In his words it was all *rubbish*. It was all wrong. He had missed the mark; he was not serving God at all. He was persecuting the Christ!

This proud man was humbled, literally, to the dust. It must have been a sickening moment for Paul. All his greatest personal achievements amounted to absolutely nothing. He was staring at the proof—and it literally blinded him.

Up to this point, Paul's whole life had been consumed with excelling in his pursuit of religion—zealously obeying the Law and doing all he could to impose it and, if necessary, physically enforcing it on others. He was a committed follower of Judaism. In this, he was a great success. He thought he was doing God's work. But now he realized it was a dead end. This was not the path that led to favor with God.

It was a path that was filled with all kinds of truth <u>about</u> God, but never actually led <u>to</u> God. It was a path of religion, of rituals, of earning God's favor with zeal and good deeds—unwilling or unable to see that it was a treadmill that never produced what the gospel of Jesus Christ offers, namely, LIFE—a changed life, a transformed life, and a life that was able to have a personal relationship with God Himself.

> "I have come that they may have **life**, and that they may have it more abundantly" (*New King James Version,* John 10:10b).

Earlier in His ministry, Jesus had given a stinging rebuke to religious Jews like Paul. In the Gospel of John, Jesus told them:

"You search the Scriptures because *you think* that in them you have eternal **life**; it is these that testify about Me; and you are *unwilling* to come to Me so that you may have **life**" (John 5:39-40).

What is Jesus saying here? **He is saying that salvation is in a person, not merely in truth.** The Christian is one whose faith is in the person who <u>IS</u> the truth.

The point here is that religious zeal and attempting to do "good works" is <u>not</u> a winning strategy when it comes to gaining favor with God—or eternal life. There is only one winning strategy and that is simple, child-like trust in Jesus Christ to save me. That faith opens the floodgates of God's blessings in Christ.

The apostle Paul sums it up powerfully in I Corinthians 1:21:

"For since in the wisdom of God the world through its wisdom did not come to know God, God was well-pleased through the foolishness of the message preached to save those who believe."

All the blessings of heaven become ours when we place our whole-hearted trust in Jesus Christ for salvation.

It is important to note also that we are saved *by* grace *through* faith. Faith is the mechanism, the means by which we are saved. It is **not** the power of God. The power that saves is not our faith; faith did not die for us—the power is in the <u>object</u> of our faith—Jesus Christ, the risen Son of God. It is not faith in our faith, but faith in Jesus Christ that saves. Our faith unites us to the One who, risen from the grave, is "the power of God unto salvation..." (Romans 1:16). Jesus Christ saves us through faith.

How then does saving faith manifest itself? Is it just an intellectual assent to the basic truths of Christianity—that Christ died for our sins, was buried, and rose again on the third day? Many believe these fundamental truths, but their lives are untouched by them. How can this be possible?

What is often missed in the modern gospel presentation is the third essential of a true saving experience of the gospel of Jesus Christ, namely, the New Birth—the divine beginning of a new life, an eternal life, a Holy Spirit-empowered life that believers share with Jesus Christ.

Jesus said, "You must be born again" (John 3:7b).

Saving faith always results in a new birth into a new life. But how do we know we have it? What are the signs of this new life?

THE ASSURANCE OF FAITH: THE NEW BIRTH

Repentance manifests visible *fruits*. As mentioned earlier, it is a change of mind which results in a change of action and/or purpose. But a change of mind about what?

About the path we were on, about the sin in our lives, about the purely selfish ambitions, goals, and purposes that consume our lives. When John the Baptist saw the Pharisees coming out to be baptized, he was not impressed. Nothing had changed in their minds or their lives, and getting baptized would have no meaning for them. True repentance produces fruit in the life.

Faith also has its fruit. It is the new birth. The new birth is the undeniable fruit of faith. Without it there is no life and therefore, there is no salvation.

"He who has the Son has the life; he who does not have the Son of God does <u>not</u> have the life" (I John 5:12).

The moment a person repents and puts his or her whole-hearted trust in Jesus Christ, at that very moment, God (in the words of Scripture) makes him or her *"alive in Christ,"* that is, He causes that person to be *born again.* They begin a new life with a new heart and a new spirit—a new purpose now directs their life. They have a new desire to live for Him who died and rose again for them. Hear Paul's words to us:

"For if we live, we live for the Lord, or if we die, we die for the Lord; therefore whether we live or die, we are the Lord's. For to this end Christ died and lived again, that He might be Lord both of the dead and of the living." (Romans 14:8-9)

"For the love of Christ controls us, having concluded this, that one died for all, therefore all died; and He died for all, so that they who live might no longer live for themselves, but for Him who died and rose again on their behalf."

(2 Corinthians 5:14-15)

How is this "new birth" accomplished?

The moment a person puts his trust in Jesus Christ, God causes His Holy Spirit (the same Spirit that dwelt in Christ Jesus) to come and dwell in the new believer. With the Holy Spirit, a new heart, a new desire to know God, and a new spiritual awareness (a new capacity to know God) that the person never had before, comes to life in him.

Somehow, this truly life-transforming experience seems lost in most presentations of the gospel today. Yet, it is this life-transforming reality that is the visible proof of saving faith. Only the life that is being transformed into the image of Christ is the life that has been born again and is now destined to spend eternity with the Lord—and no other. Jesus made this clear to Nicodemus in John 3. Paul also confirmed it in Romans 8:

> "However, you are not in the flesh but in the Spirit, if indeed the Spirit of God dwells in you. But if anyone does not have the Spirit of Christ, he does not belong to Him" (Romans 8:9).

Countless Scriptures testify to this glorious truth: Romans 6:4, 8:9-11; I Corinthians 15:45, 49; 2 Corinthians 5:17; Galatians 2:20; 2 Timothy 1:8-10, 13-14; 1 Peter 1:3-9; 2 Peter 1:3-11....and many, many more.

Yet there remains this sobering, solemn fact. Jesus says:

> "...Strait is the gate and narrow is the way that leads to <u>life</u>, and <u>few</u> are those who find it" (King James Version, Matthew 7:14).

How can this be? The simple answer is because men fail to obey the gospel call. And why so few? Because most will refuse to come. But why? We'll see the answer in the next section.

Long my imprisoned spirit lay

Fast bound in sin and nature's night

Thine eye diffused a quickening ray,

I woke, the dungeon flamed with light;

My chains fell off, my heart was free;

I rose, went forth and followed Thee.

—*Charles Wesley*

Questions for the Huddle

1. Both repentance and faith are essential to salvation? Why?

2. The essence of faith is trust. How is this different from just believing the facts about the death, burial, and resurrection of Jesus Christ?

3. The apostle Paul declared that he knew "<u>whom</u> he had believed" not "<u>what</u> he had believed." What is the difference?

4. The undeniable proof of faith is the new birth. What happens when a person is "born again"?

5. The new birth is the beginning of a new life in which we are transformed from being men and women who are "dead in our sins" and enemies of God, into men and women who are like Christ in mind, soul, and spirit. Why should being "born again" give us assurance of our faith and salvation?

Notes

_____

_____

_____

_____

_____

_____

_____

_____

_____

_____

_____

_____

_____

_____

_____

_____

_____

_____

_____

_____

_____

_____

The Gospel "Call"

It is written... "Come, Follow Me."
There is no Plan B.

Matthew 19:21

The Gospel "Call"

HIS CALL: "COME, FOLLOW ME!"

There is only one way to God and that is through faith in Jesus Christ. His invitation is made to all men. He does not wish for any "to perish but for all to come to repentance" (2 Peter 3:9b). But most men will reject this offer. Why?

Because it will seem like too high a price to follow Him. But, how can that be? Isn't salvation "free"?

It is free in the sense that you can do absolutely nothing to earn it or deserve it. And it is free in the sense that it is a gift from God to those who choose to repent and put their whole-hearted faith and trust in Jesus Christ (Mark 1:15). This is all gloriously true—this makes it simple enough even for a child to be saved.

Yet in three different gospels, Jesus says (without apology), "If any man wishes to come after Me, let him deny himself, take up his cross and follow Me" (Mark 8:34).

Wow! Talk about throwing down the gauntlet. That doesn't sound so easy, does it? That's the point. God has made the possibility of salvation simple, but not easy.

The beginning of the Lord's call to every one of us who chooses to follow Him is the call to **"take up the cross."** It is the core truth of repentance. It's the beginning point of the only path that leads to life.

Everyone in the Roman world of Jesus and Paul's day knew that the command, "take up your cross," meant only one thing: death. When the Roman soldier arrived at your door and told you to take up your cross, you knew that your life in this world was over. You had no choice.

Jesus makes the same demand on each of His followers. The big difference is that you have a choice. You can choose to obey the command or reject it. The good news is that this "death" leads to life—spiritual life, eternal life. But to reject the command is to reject Him and His offer of salvation.

Some would try to make an artificial distinction at this point between a *believer* and a *disciple*. However, the New Testament offers no such distinction. The Bible only uses the term believer in contrast with an **<u>un</u>**believer, never a disciple.

It was the *disciples* who were the followers of Christ (and they were all born-again believers)—the Bible says it was the <u>disciples</u> who were first called Christians at Antioch.

You can no more separate believing in Christ from following Christ, than you can separate the first breath in a new-born child's life from the rest of the breaths he will take during his entire life. You can distinguish them, but not separate them. If the child takes his first breath, but then doesn't breathe for an hour, what happens? It dies. The same is true of a profession of faith which does not result in the "believer" following Christ.

To summarize Martyn Lloyd-Jones:

> You can distinguish justification from sanctification theologically, but you cannot separate them in a _practical_ sense—justification, sanctification, and glorification are all part of one true salvation experience. (See <u>Studies in John 17</u>, _The Assurance of Salvation_, p. 374; Crossway Books, Wheaton, IL 2000.)

In Matthew 16:24-26, Jesus exposes the conflict that will arise in the hearts of most people when they are faced with the true gospel. What is it?

For many (most?) people, their lives in <u>this</u> world appear too attractive, too compelling, and filled with too many opportunities to believe it's not real. They are blinded by the devil's delusion of lasting wealth, success, and opportunity in this life. The key word is _lasting_.

A message which has been endlessly promoted to our culture, especially our young people, is: "You can have it all in this life if you work hard and want it badly enough." It is all a complete fraud! How do we know?

Jesus exposes the true deception of it all when He says:

> "For whoever wishes to save his life (in this world) will **lose** it; but whoever **loses** his life for My sake will **find** it" (Matthew 16:26a).

Then comes this sobering word of explanation:

> "For what will a man be profited, if he gains the
> whole world, and **forfeits** his soul?" (Matthew
> 16:26).

The question is meant to be rhetorical, that is, the answer
is revealed by understanding the question.

It does a person <u>no</u> good at all if they *gain the <u>whole</u> world*
and then they die! That is the hidden *deception* of the opportunity which this world system offers. You can't take the
world or whatever you have gained in this world with you—
it's all a delusion! In the end, you have gained nothing. Not
only will you have wasted your life—much more im-
portantly, you will have wasted the only opportunity you
will ever have to be reconciled to God and find eternal life.

THE CROSS THAT CRUCIFIES...FREES!

Once you die and leave this world behind, you have nothing
to offer God to atone for your sin and rebellion. You are
doomed and condemned. That is why the message of the
cross as the "first thing" is so crucial.

It is important to note that this message is to the sinner. The sinner's path to life begins with death. It
began with Jesus' death for us and *then* begins to come
to life IN US when we, by faith, turn to follow Him.

That is why the apostle Paul said in Galatians 2:20a:

> "I have been crucified with Christ; and it is no
> longer I who live, but Christ lives in me; and the

life which I now live in the flesh I live by faith in the Son of God..."

But how do we truly know if we are one of those "few" who find the "narrow gate" and enter it? How can we be sure we have found the gate? The answer is simple. We will hear His voice. He <u>is</u> the gate! Then we follow Him.

> "**I am** the door; if anyone enters through Me, he will be saved..." (John 10:9a).

> "My sheep hear my voice, and I know them, and they follow Me; and I give eternal life to them, and they shall never perish; and no one shall snatch them out of My hand." (John 10:27-28)

NOTE: *Do you wonder if He is calling you? If you are reading this book, then there is NO doubt that Jesus is calling <u>you</u> to follow Him! That much is certain. The only question is whether you, after hearing His call, will choose to follow Him. From this point on, there will never be a question that you had a chance to choose life—Eternal Life.*

But the first step to following Him is the call to die. "If any man wishes to come after Me, let him deny himself, take up his cross and follow Me" (Matthew 16:24).

To follow Christ <u>is</u> to leave the *broad way*; to follow Christ <u>is</u> to turn to the *narrow way*. His way <u>is</u> to "deny yourself"— to say NO to all the potential with which the world system is tempting you. It may be the lust for personal wealth and success, or a hundred other dreams or goals you see as your primary purpose in this life.

Your goal, as a follower of Christ, is to glorify Him with your life...and He will give you all the wealth and success you need to accomplish <u>that</u> purpose...and you will also have "treasure in heaven" as well! (2 Corinthians 5:15).

What is Jesus saying?

He is saying that if you want the benefits of his cross (his atoning death and his life-giving resurrection) in your life, then you are going to have to die as well. Not physically, but die to <u>your</u> goals and dreams and selfish ambitions.

It will mean turning from going your way to go His way (Isaiah 53, Romans 3)

Why? Why does He demand this of all of us?

It is because He knows these are the things that will hold you back from following Him with all your heart. You can't bring them on the narrow path to His kingdom, the Kingdom of God. Letting those things go will seem hard at first, almost like dying. But you will soon find that once you do, you will experience a freedom you could never have known.

Will you end up without goals and true purpose in life? Not at all! Christ will give you new goals and an entirely new purpose in life—one that will have eternal value and lasting rewards. You will have <u>His</u> goals and fulfill <u>His</u> purpose for your life. What will that look like?

The specifics will be different for each person. But they will all revolve around the same ultimate goal and purpose that guided His life when He walked the earth—the same purpose for which He came. What was that purpose? "To seek and save that which was lost" and to glorify the Father, "having accomplished the work which Thou hast given Me to do" (Luke 19:10; John 17:4b)

THE GOSPEL "CALL" · 73

It will also mean a continuing life of "denying yourself and taking up your cross...__daily__" (Luke 9:23b). We begin with the cross, and we live by the cross. It is the only way to keep God's Holy Spirit free to work in us and neutralize the awesome power of the flesh to lure us back into the path of sin.

The apostle Paul followed in His footsteps:

> "Now I rejoice in my sufferings for your sake, and in my flesh I do my share on behalf of His body, which is the church, in filling up what is lacking in Christ's afflictions... that I might fully carry out the preaching of the word of God..."(Colossians 1:24, 25b)—with the goal of saving the lost.

> "We proclaim Him, admonishing every man and teaching every man with all wisdom, so that we may present every man complete in Christ" (Colossians 1:28).

Paul's ultimate mission in life was simple. Share the gospel with every person and disciple those who respond in faith until they are conformed to the image of Christ.

THE DELUSION OF THE WORLD'S CALL

But you will never turn away from all the world offers unless and until you see that it is really all a delusion—and that the offer is not real! It can't be real. How do you know? **You are going to die!** And all that you have supposedly "gained" will die with you.

The Scriptures are clear:

"As for man, his days are like grass; as a flower of the field, so he flourishes. When the wind has passed over it, it is no more, and its place acknowledges it no longer" (Psalms 103:15-16).

"For the sun rises with a scorching wind and withers the grass; and its flower falls off and the beauty of its appearance is <u>destroyed</u>; so too the rich man **in the midst of his pursuits** will fade away" (James 1:11).

"ALL FLESH IS LIKE GRASS, AND ALL ITS GLORY LIKE THE FLOWER OF GRASS. THE GRASS WITHERS, AND THE FLOWER FALLS OFF, BUT THE WORD OF THE LORD ENDURES FOREVER. And this is the word which was preached to you" (1 Peter 1:24-25).

The apostle James minces no words when he declares:

"Yet you do not know what your life will be like tomorrow. You are just a <u>vapor</u> that appears for a little while and then <u>vanishes</u> away" (James 4:14).

The pioneer missionary, C.T. Studd, summed up this truth when he said,

We only have one life, and it will soon be past. Only what's done for Christ will last.

Even if your personal goals are religious, they can be as selfish and worldly as any other. If the motive is not to glorify Christ, something is wrong. It means you are on the wrong path or about to make a wrong decision.

That is what the apostle Paul found in Christ and it totally transformed him—he truly became a "new creation" and everyone saw it.

Following Christ became Paul's consuming passion; he lived to know Him intimately and to do His Father's will. His life was spent finishing the work which Christ had begun—to seek and save the lost. Eventually, this becomes the passion of every born-again believer.

The problem is we don't hear this message very often today. Where did this part of the gospel message disappear to???

Is it possible that this is the reason the church seems to be irrelevant to so many today? Is it possible that this is why the gospel has so little apparent impact on our culture? We think so.

THE GOSPEL TODAY

The Bible is still here and it still declares that "the gospel is the power of God unto salvation." Yet it clearly does not seem to have the impact that it did for the first three hundred years after Christ died and rose again. Why? What is missing?

The problem is the <u>unchanged</u> life. The "gospel" often heard today would have us believe that a person can receive the gift of salvation by faith, and the omnipotent God, who created the heavens and the earth with a word and raised Jesus from the dead, can invade the life of an ungodly rebel, forgive him of all his sin and rebellion, cause him to be born again and indwelt by God's own divine Spirit—and that life **not** be changed! Seriously?!?

Nothing could be more at odds with what the Bible declares to be the truth about a born again follower of Christ. Paul states unequivocally that "if any man is in Christ, he is a new creature (i.e., a new <u>creation</u>—not a person who has been reformed, but a person that never existed before!); the old things passed away; behold, new things have come" (2 Corinthians 5:17).

What are these "new" things? What does this "new life" look like? The Bible says,

First, we will be "<u>transformed</u> by the renewing of our minds" (Romans 12:2).

Second, the Scriptures also say that the born again child of God is "being <u>conformed</u> to the image of His Son" (Romans 8:29).

We will see what this means in the next section.

Jesus calls us; o'er the tumult

Of our life's wild, restless sea,

Day by day His sweet voice sounds,

Saying, "Christian, follow Me."

Jesus calls us from the worship

Of the vain world's golden store:

From each idol that would keep us,

Saying, "Christian, love me more."

—Mrs. C. F. Alexander

Questions for the Huddle

1. Why does the gospel "call" begin with the command to "deny yourself, take up your cross, and follow Him (Christ)?"

2. The world system will try to lure you into believing that you can have lasting wealth, success and prosperity in this world.

    A. What is the deception in this offer?

    B. How do you know?

3. If you have lived your life for your sake, doing what you want to do, trying to fulfill your goals, plans and dreams for your life on this earth, and then die—but do not really know God and have no "treasure" in heaven, what will you have gained for all your efforts?

4. The Bible says, "It is appointed to man once to die, and then the judgment" (Hebrews 9:27). If you have read this book, when you stand before God, will you have any defense for your decision if you refuse to repent and follow the Lord?

5. What does it mean that in order to follow Christ, you must turn from the "broad way" to the "narrow way"? What changes will you have to make in your life to do this?

6. If you choose to follow Christ, what will the purpose of your life be?

Notes

The Transformed Life

"Therefore if any man is in Christ, he is a new creature; the old things have passed away; Behold, new things have come."

2 Corinthians 5:17

The Transformed Life

TRUTH THROUGH A TRANSFORMED LIFE

The most powerful weapon that the Church of Jesus Christ has in the fulfilling of His mission to "seek and save the lost" and "to make disciples of all nations" is the truth of the gospel revealed in a life that has been transformed by it. "Christ in you" is not only the foundation of the Christian's eternal security, it is the ultimate weapon in the battle for men's souls. The truth of the Gospel revealed in a life cannot be easily denied.

The Scriptures highlight the two primary goals that will dominate and characterize our "new life" in Christ as we grow and mature as Christians.

First, we will be "<u>transformed</u> by the renewing of our minds" (Romans 12:2). What does this mean?

It means that the more we know and understand and embrace the truths of God's Word, the more we will become like God in our character, in our motives, and in our purpose for life. The enabling and empowering work of the Holy Spirit within us is essential to accomplishing this transformation into Christ-likeness.

Second, the Scriptures also say that the born-again child of God is "being <u>conformed</u> to the image of His Son" (Romans 8:29). What does this mean?

It means that rather than having our goals and desires "shaped" by the world system and the god of this world, we are more and more each day seeing the world as Jesus Christ sees it—and desiring to see it delivered from the darkness that prevails over it. In the Word of God and the Spirit of God, we have the "mind of Christ."

The more we know Him and learn of Him, the more we will think like Him and be like Him. This too is the fruit of the Holy Spirit's work in us.

Having said that, the change doesn't happen all at once any more than a new born baby becomes an adult overnight—it is a process, a life-long process.

Theologians call it *sanctification.* The root word means to be holy, to be set apart for a special purpose. In the case of the Christian, it means to be set apart to God and for the purposes of God in your life.

Just as our human transformation from infant to adult is often in many ways dramatic, it is the same in our spiritual growth. But at other times it occurs more slowly and subtly. Regardless, there are clear indications whether life is really there or not. Dead people are different from live people—and live people know the difference!

Likewise, spiritually dead people are different from those who are spiritually alive. There are "signs" of life.

What are some of the signs of "life"? What are some of the biblically-based signs that God is at work in a life?

As we said above, the process occurs over time and will vary in speed and intensity with each person. It is also true that there are times when the Spirit of God is doing something *within* our souls that cannot be seen on the outside—and sometimes this "soul surgery" can be some of the deepest spiritual work in our lives.

> Hebrews 12:6 says, "For those whom the Lord loves He *disciplines*, and He scourges every son whom He receives."

Discipline is a sign of life, <u>not</u> of death.

In other words, what is given here is for each of us to use to gauge God's work in **our** own lives, not in the lives of others.

Only the power of God "by the Spirit," can accomplish God's work. Too often well-meaning Christians try to do God's work for Him. He doesn't need our help! Remember, He is God...we are not God!

You cannot see into another person's heart, nor can they see into yours. Unless a person is engaged in blatantly sinful behavior, normally your part will be to pray for them and offer loving encouragement to seek God. It takes real spiritual sensitivity to know when to speak and when not to. When you do speak, let your words always be "seasoned with grace," kindness, and love.

THE "SIGNS" OF NEW LIFE

The apostle Paul wrote,

> "Therefore we have been buried with Him through baptism into death, so that as Christ was raised from the dead through the glory of the Father, <u>so we too might walk in newness of life</u>" (Romans 6:4).

The Christian life is a "new" life—literally, the word means <u>**new**</u> in the sense that it has **never existed before**; it is a new <u>kind</u> of life—it's a Spirit-empowered life—a life empowered by God's Holy Spirit. We have been made partakers of God's divine nature in Christ (2 Peter 1:3-4).

The list below is not intended to be an exhaustive list, but it does give a solid starting point to the things God works into a life which He has truly caused to be born again. The idea that a person can be "born from above," indwelt by the eternal, omnipotent God—and there be no change—simply does not square with the Bible's description of it.

The "New Man" in Christ—

- Has a thankful heart. He knows he did not earn or deserve God's redemption or forgiveness and he is consciously and eternally grateful (Romans 1:21; 1 Thessalonians 5:18; Hebrews 13:15; Luke 17:17).
- Has a new love for God and Christ (Romans. 5:5;

1 Corinthians 8:3; John 16:27; I John 4:7).

- Has a new desire and power to turn from sin and resist temptation (Romans 8:12-14).
- Has a new love and hunger for the truth of God's word (1 Peter 2:2; 2 Thessalonians 2:10; Proverbs 6:23; Psalm 19:8).
- Has a new desire to love God and demonstrates that love by obeying His commands (John 14:23; Romans 5:5).
- Has a new purpose in life. He lives to know and do the will of God (Mark 3:35; Ephesians 6:6; 1 Peter 4:2; 1 John 2:17).
- Has a new love for the brethren. They are now "family" to him (1 Peter 1:22; 1 Thessalonians 4:9; Hebrews 13:1; 1 John 4:7, 11-12, 21, 5:2-3).
- Has a new passion in his life—to know God (Philippians 3:8-10).
- Has a new power working in his life to produce godliness and Christ-likeness, the fruit of His indwelling Holy Spirit (Colossians 1:3-14; Philippians 1:6, 2:12-13; Galatians 5:22-25; 2 Peter 1:2-11).

These are some of the "signs of life" in a Christian, in a life that has turned from sin to following Christ. These signs will be manifested—in a greater or lesser degree—depending on how much God's perfecting, sanctifying work has been accomplished in the individual's life.

They are as much an indication of what God desires to do in a life as they are a measure of what He has accomplished. The Lord Jesus said in the Sermon on the Mount, "Blessed are those who hunger and thirst for righteousness, for they shall be satisfied." He also told us to "Seek first the kingdom of God and His righteousness..." (Matthew. 5:6, 6:33).

These verses contain both a promise and an imperative. They are meant to be the guiding principles of our new life in Christ.

To follow Him <u>is</u> to seek His kingdom; to follow Him <u>is</u> to seek righteousness.

The Lord has promised that to those who follow Him "He <u>will</u> give eternal life."

The good news is He promised that "if we seek Him with all our heart, we <u>will</u> find Him"—not just truth about God, we will find God Himself.

> *Eternal life is not meant to be just a truth we know about, it is meant to be a life we experience—a life we begin to experience now—and continue to enjoy forever (Read John 17:3).*

"WHAT MUST I DO TO BE SAVED?"

This is a famous—and extremely important—question. It is also important to understand it in its context. Hopefully, after reading this book, you will have a greater appreciation of its importance.

The Philippian jailer asked this question in Acts 16:30. The rich young ruler asked the same basic question (and the response of the Lord Jesus is recorded in Matthew 19, Mark 10, and Luke 18). Are the answers different? Yes and no. But what is important to understand is that Jesus' answers led each individual to the place they needed to be in order to be saved. He knew them personally, and He knew what the obstacle was that would keep them from trusting Him, believing Him, and following Him.

Paul's answer to the jailer in Acts 16:31 was simple, "Believe in the Lord Jesus Christ, and you shall be saved..." But what about the Lord's answer to the rich young ruler?

His response in Luke 18:22 seems like it was very, very different. He said, "Go, sell all that you possess, and distribute it to the poor, and you shall have treasure in heaven; and come, follow Me."

How can this be the same path to salvation? We know that in both cases the ultimate issue was to enable them to put their faith and trust in Jesus Christ for their salvation. The key to the difference was the Lord's recognition of the obstacle(s) that needed to be removed in order for them to be able to put their trust in Jesus Christ for salvation.

For the Philippian jailer, there were no obstacles. He was a dead man. Nothing had a hold on him, he had nothing to give up. Guarding Paul was his sole responsibility. If Paul escaped or anything happened to him, he would forfeit his life.

For the rich, young ruler, the gospel message sounded very different. It was going to require a soul-searching sacrifice, at least in his mind. He was very, very rich and he had a good life. He saw nothing wrong with his life—he actually believed he was "right with God"—he just wasn't sure he had "eternal life," and he wanted to make sure he added that to his pile of earthly treasures.

When Jesus told him he had to give up all he had earned and accumulated in this life in order to be saved, he was stunned! But Jesus was just exposing the real gods in his life–covetousness, greed, and pride. He was proud of all that he had accomplished; he felt he was a great success, he lived an apparently moral life, and he "kept the commandments."

He had no clue that in reality he was the prisoner of his riches and prosperity. He didn't own them, they owned him. Jesus exposed it.

The problem was—he loved his prison! He didn't want to leave. Life, his life in this world, was good. Ultimately, Jesus' question to the rich young ruler was this: Which do you want more, your riches or Me?

The Scriptures say that the rich, young ruler was "sad"—which means he clearly understood the choice—but He chose the riches. That is why in the next verse it says, "...Jesus looked (right) at him and said, 'How hard it is for those who are wealthy to enter the kingdom of God!'"

Jesus was revealing that, in reality, he was **not** right with God...and had no treasure in <u>heaven</u>. In order to be saved he would have to "turn from his idol," let his riches go and then he would be free to put his trust in the One who alone could be his Savior. Was he giving up anything of lasting value? No. But to him it seemed like an enormous cost, a price he was unwilling to pay.

The point here is that the gospel addresses the need of every person—right where they are. God knows the heart of each of us. He knows what the obstacles are to putting our whole-hearted faith and trust in Jesus Christ. Jesus was resolute when He said, "A man cannot serve two masters."

The divided heart cannot exercise saving faith in Christ. When we hear the true gospel, the whole gospel, the Holy

Spirit will reveal to each of us what it will mean in our lives to leave the old life behind, to turn off the "broad way" and follow the Lord on the narrow way. While we may give up some apparent potential for success in this life, He offers us a share in the kingdom and glory of God forever. To the enlightened heart, there is no comparison...and there is no sacrifice.

When we share the gospel with a lost soul, we don't know what obstacles lie in the path to faith, obstacles that must be removed. But that is not our job. It's the job of the Holy Spirit. He alone is the One who convicts a person of his or her sin, the things which bind them in this life and the judgment they face if they do not turn from them. He will reveal it to them. Our job is simply to present the whole gospel—and the great salvation that it makes possible for those who repent and believe the gospel (Hebrew 4:12-13; John 16:7-13).

> "This is eternal life, that they may know You, the only true God, and Jesus Christ whom You have sent" (John 17:3).

"...THE LIFE I NOW LIVE" (GALATIONS 2:20)

We began this journey through the gospel with the question that each of us must answer: "Are you going to die?"

That question is meant to put everything in true perspective—to reveal what really matters in this life. Jesus said, **"What does it profit a man if he gains the whole world, but loses his soul?"** (Matthew 16:26).

The answer is, there is no profit at all—it is all a total deception created by Satan ("the god of this world"). A deception so cunning and so compelling that when we die we will find (to our eternal loss) that we have wasted the real opportunity and purpose of this life: to glorify God.

Now the choice is yours. What are you going to do? Whom will you follow?

When the Lord asked Peter if he wanted to turn back like so many others, Peter said, "Lord to whom shall we go, You have the words of eternal life" (John 6:68).

Do you believe that? If the Lord asked you the same question, how would you respond? Would your life back up your response?

As Hebrews 2:3 poses the critical question, "How will we escape if we neglect so great a salvation?" The answer is: You won't escape. No one does. How do we know?

> "It is appointed unto man once to die, and after this comes judgment" (Hebrews 9:27).

Do you hear His voice calling? **He says, "Come, follow Me."** **There is no Plan B.**

Now you have to choose.

I heard the voice of Jesus say –
"I am this dark world's Light;
Look unto Me, thy morn shall rise,
And all thy day be bright."

I looked to Jesus, and I found
In Him my Star, my Sun;
And in that Light of life I'll walk
Till traveling days are done.

—Horatius Bonar

Questions for the Huddle

1. The most effective weapon the church of Jesus Christ has in "seeking and saving the lost" is the truth of the gospel seen in a life transformed by the gospel. How are we transformed? (Romans 12:1).

2. What does it mean to have a "renewed" mind?

3. What does it mean to be "conformed" to the image of God's Son?

4. Dead people don't know they are dead. Dead people don't change. People who are alive know they are alive and prove it by showing "signs of life". Are you alive?

5. The born again follower of Christ has a "new" life—a life he never experienced before. What are some "signs" of this "new" life in a Christian?

6. What must you do to be saved?

7. Do you have any idols in your life which are keeping you from following Christ with a whole heart?

8. What will it profit you if you fulfill all your goals and dreams and desires in this life—then die and go to hell?

Notes

_____

_____

_____

_____

_____

_____

_____

_____

_____

_____

_____

_____

_____

_____

_____

_____

_____

_____

_____

_____

_____

_____

IRON-MAN CHRISTIANITY

SUNDAY DISCIPLESHIP EVENT

BREAKFAST WITH CHAMPIONS: ATHLETE TESTIMONIES & FELLOWSHIP

SESSION #1

A LIFE THAT MATTERS

SESSION #2

"FOLLOW ME." THERE IS NO PLAN B.

FOR MORE INFO: CONTACT WALLACE FRANÇIS
770-980-2020   EMAIL: info@afci.us

WHY HAVE AN IMC SUNDAY EVENT?

LOOKING TO START/RE-ENERGIZE A MEN'S DISCIPLESHIP MINISTRY IN YOUR CHURCH?

- *SPEAK TO YOUR MEN IN A LANGUAGE THEY UNDERSTAND.*
- *COMMUNICATE THROUGH CONCEPTS THEY ALREADY BELIEVE AND ACCEPT.*
- *SPORTS IS THE UNIVERSAL LANGUAGE OF MEN!*
- *SPORTS EMBRACES ALL THE ESSENTIAL FUNDAMENTALS OF CHRISTIAN DISCIPLESHIP:*

AUTHORITY ♦ TRUST ♦ SACRIFICE ♦ FAITHFULNESS
DILIGENCE ♦ DISCIPLINE ...AND MUCH MORE.

DISCIPLESHIP IS THE <u>ONLY</u> WINNING STRATEGY THAT THE LORD GIVES US.

"Run in such a way that you may win."
1 CORINTHIANS 9:24

36296320R00065

Made in the USA
San Bernardino, CA
19 July 2016